HE AND I

HE AND I

EMMANUEL
MOSES

translated by
MARILYN
HACKER

Oberlin College Press
FIELD Translation Series
Oberlin, Ohio

The FIELD Translation Series, vol. 29
Oberlin College Press, 50 N. Professor Street, Oberlin, OH 44074

www.oberlin.edu/ocpress

Cover image: Keren Benbenisty

Cover design: Steve Farkas

Library of Congress Cataloging-in-Publication Data

Moses, Emmanuel, 1960-
[Poems. English. Selections]
He and I / Emmanuel Moses ; translated by Marilyn Hacker.
p. cm. — (The Field translation series ; v. 29)
ISBN-13: 978-0-932440-37-2 (pbk. : alk. paper)
ISBN-10: 0-932440-37-1 (pbk. : alk. paper)
I. Hacker, Marilyn. II. Title.
PQ2673.O69A6 2009
841'.914—dc22

2009031031

Contents

Translator's Introduction

Emmanuel Moses was born in Casablanca in 1959, the son of a French-educated German Jew and a French Jew of Polish descent: one an historian of philosophy and the other a painter. He spent his early childhood in France, lived from the age of ten until his mid-twenties in Israel, where he studied history at the Hebrew University of Jerusalem, and then returned to Paris, where he still lives. He is the author of eight collections of poems, most recently *D'un perpetuel hiver* (Gallimard, 2009) and *Figure rose* (Flammarion, 2006, which received one of the annual *Prix de poésie* from the Académie Française), and of eight novels and collections of short fiction. Another poetry collection, *L'Animal,* is already scheduled for publication. Fluent in four languages, Moses is a translator into French of contemporary Hebrew fiction and poetry, notably of Yehuda Amichai and, recently, Agi Mishol; he edited anthologies of modern poetry in Hebrew for the publishers Obsidiane and Gallimard. He also translates from the German and from the English, including C. K. Williams, Raymond Carver, and younger poets like the recent National Poetry Series winner Donna Stonecipher. The poems translated here, written between 2004 and 2008, are from *Figure rose*, *D'un perpetuel hiver*, and *L'Animal.*

A polyglot whose experience of the world comes as much from travel and human intercourse as from books, from an interrogation of the past which coexists with his experience of the present, Emmanuel Moses is a kind of *poète sans frontières*. While some contemporary French poets eschew geographical specificity, a perennial subject of Moses' poems is the crossing and the porosity of actual borders, geographical and temporal. A (Proustian?) train of thought set in motion by the placement of a park bench, the stripe of sunlight on a brick wall, will move the speaker and the poem itself from Amsterdam to Jerusalem, from a boyhood memory to a 19th century chronicle, from Stendhal to the Shoah. A subtle irony permeates Moses' work, even (or especially) at moments meant to be self-reflective or romantic, an irony applied to the events of history as readily as to the events of a single young or aging man's life. It is clear in Moses' poems as in his fiction that the macro-events of "history" are made up of the miniscule events of individual existence, and that they must be perceived as such to be understood. The breadth of the poet's reading and his intimate relationship with architecture, music, and painting inform his work and populate it with unexpected interlocutors: Chopin, Buxtehude, Fragonard, Breughel—or a London barman, or a Turkish woman pharmacist.

References to diaspora and displacement, to individual histories involving plural geographies and languages, are ubiquitous in this collection. Moses creates a fluidity of time as well as place as these texts move across the Europe of his imagination: Napoleon's invasion of Slovenia, the Palazzo Farnese (which currently houses the French Embassy in Rome), the death of Chopin, even the Crucifixion, come into focus. The quintessentially cosmopolitan Istanbul is the setting for what seems to be an amorous idyll; Majorca becomes the impetus for a retrospective reflection on cultures crossing in transit. "Letters from Brandenburg"—the state surrounding Berlin, identified with Bach—illustrates Moses' geographical and temporal jump-cutting, as its six sections (mirroring the concertos?) move from childhood recollection to reflections on human communication to the abrupt, oblique description of a pogrom. As well as recalling Bach, Brandenburg was the site of the imprisonment by the Germans of the French Résistant poet André Frénaud, who published a series of "Poèmes de Brandebourg" written during his incarceration between 1940-1942. The work of Frénaud, who died in 1993, is a touchstone for Moses, and most French readers would see Frénaud as one recipient of these "Letters." Berlin's history haunts the lovers' bed in "Royal Blue" as well. The "Riverbend Passage" sequence is at once more lyric and linguistically ludic, though in a minor key and somber tone.

Reading it, and, even more, translating it, I could perceive it as an homage to or dialogue with another Jewish poet without borders, Paul Celan.

The fluid and ironic "Mr. Nobody" persona first appeared briefly in a 2003 collection, to which he gave the title *Dernières nouvelles de Monsieur Néant*. He reappears at much greater length in a sequence of these more recent poems. "Néant" can be translated as "Nothingness," as in the Englishing of Sartre's doorstopper. But "Nothingness" is a doorstopper of a word all by itself in English: after reading a half-dozen or more poems about him, Emmanuel Moses' persona emerges as much more of an "everyman / no man" than an avatar of the existential void. He seems to me to be present even in poems that don't bear his name, "Small i," for example, and, in a register finally eschewing self-mockery, "Towards Buxtehude." He is a Chaplinesque (even Woody Allen-esque, and, why not, a touch of Joseph Roth in the Hôtel Tournon?) reassessment of the diasporic, elegiac, and history-haunted speaker of many of the other poems: disappointed in love, allergic to most of humanity, but endlessly rewriting a play for myriad characters in a series of temporary residences.

Moses cultivates a formal fluidity in his poems. Some, in French as in translation, are fairly straightforward open-form lyrics or narratives, which may on occasion ("On Ugliness" is an example) open a "frame story" only to veer away and out of the frame. Other poems incorporate prose passages, or are made up of pared, short, near-syllabic stanzas. Some are deliberately, enigmatically fragmentary. On the subject of this choice, he has written:

> For me, the fragment is something that has been torn off. This violence is at the heart of the writing process, or so I feel. It is a displacement and also a dislocation. What is being created thus? A kind of golem, brimming with destructive powers. You still feel the phantom entity from which the scrap has been detached. The result is a text containing pain and a fool-

ish hope for a healing. I wanted to speak about the mystery contained in the fragment and the imagination it stimulates in the reader's mind but that aspect seems now to me superficial, anecdotal. The fragment is both the result of a mutilation (of the uninterrupted flow of language) and the hope for a miracle: the restoration of its lost unity.

(Interview conducted by Donna Stonecipher for chicagopostmodernpoetry.com, 2006)

Many of the poems in this collection relate, directly or indirectly, to the life and death of Stéphane Moses, the poet's father. Stéphane Moses was born in Berlin in 1931, but educated (in French) in Morocco from the age of six onwards, to pursue his university studies in France. A secular youth, from a confluence of European Jewish cultures decimated by the Shoah, he began his inquiries into Jewish tradition and philosophy when a student at the Ecole Normale Supérieure in the 1950s, as part of the "Jewish philosophical renewal" exemplified by the work of Léon Askénazi, André Neher, and Emmanuel Levinas. He became in his turn an historian and analyst of 19th and early 20th century European Jewish thought: his writings on Walter Benjamin, Kafka, Celan, Levinas, Gershom Scholem, and Franz Rosenzweig are preeminent in the field in France. He died in 2007, after years of cancer treatment. The writer son's regard and love for his scholar father permeate much of his work, but the poems written in 2006-2008 in particular address him, reflect on his history, eulogize him, and compose his elegy, from the thoughtful and ultimately celebratory "The Terrace" and "Alive" to the oblique and deranging "Funeral Supper," a sequence that seems to exemplify a description Moses gave of his own work:

the obscurity of the impulse seems to occupy an important place in the genesis, something that is veiled, that evades any precise form, a fugitive of a sort and ending in light: something has appeared, at the end of the process, has been shaped by daylight, has come to existence, to a dense and light existence…

(Interview: chicagopostmodernpoetry.com, 2006)

Moses' choice of George Herbert for an epigraph is one entrance for a reader into the disquiet of this poem: not only an acknowledgment that the most naked confrontation of the poetic imagination with the fact of death may have been that of the English poets now called Metaphysical, but an attempt to draw from and revivify the energy of that face-off.

English poets of the 17th century, Frénaud, the French Résistant mystic, Celan and his reconstitution of the contemporary lyric in a language that would always be as much inimical as native, Yehuda Amichai after years of a translator's intimacy—as well as Walter Benjamin, Victor Hugo, and a cinematic overlay of one landscape, one era, on another: these are some of the landmark reference points for Moses and thence for his readers. Yet, despite his multilingual erudition, the dizzying range of his interlocutors, and his obvious pleasure (not in the least doctrinal) in formal experimentation, Moses is a poet with a direct and almost intimate address to the reader who engages with his work: in turn wry, melancholy, funny, self-deprecating, mercurial, fraternal.

Marilyn Hacker
Paris, 2009

He and I

Small i

Small i suffers and muddles
a sky-blue thread stripes his heart
as if his eye had leaked into it

he wails he vomits himself up
little master Small i
scarlet with anger
at his intestinal torpor

a yellow broom bush by the tracks
no longer calms Small i down
nor purple shrubs the wind abandons
between glistening puddles

and yet Small i once was
complicit with the world
had all the elbow room he needed
at its all-night cafeteria

On Ugliness

Beauty underlying ugliness
is a hackneyed subject
further into the thought
one finds ugliness again
but fundamental
a hard and arid soil with nothing more to hide

this is what a redheaded girl with blue eyes writes down
on a blank page of her travel journal
she just passed a quiet night at the hotel Krasnapolsky
—fate's hotel—
she is having breakfast in the mythical winter garden
feeling chic and a bit outdated
she has a passion for William Morris
and Tiffany
establishes no hierarchy between decoration and art

Where are the frost-whitened orchards
which, two years earlier,
seemed, beneath the springtime sky
to be singing the creator's praises?
Where is the kingfisher perched delicately on a branch
whose gaze went back and forth between the pond
and the painter with an evangelist's eyes?

He is still slogging through the dawn mud
leaving the household in slumber
and then he stops in front of the rosebush at the coomb's edge
each time he repeats his miracle:
tarnishes the immaculate petals
darkens the crisp leaves

today a beetle adds its touch to the picture
its emerald becomes blank pebble
sometimes he sees his despair
as a veil
and at others
as what raises the veil

He and I

what's disturbing
is the glowing darkness
between the two rooms

in one a child pretends he's rolling
his hoop across a city

in the other a man is sitting
with his head bent towards the floor

so as not to burn his eyes

*

later the man watched the child
score a point while expecting
the white-gloved waiter
who'd bring him his bowl of raspberries
on a bed of ice
neither of the two was happy
or unhappy

It's Late, Miss China

the cause of despair was
the effect of another despair

the erased world still pulsed
raindrops   ants
a world dreamed henceforth
across the snow

*

and after weeks of insomnia
the dream, at last

reeds   smoke
a soldier in rags

*

little gnat
in the grimy windowpane
my silence and my stillness
finally frighten you
and you fly away

*

the car's headlights
coming through the fog
at full speed
interested him so much that

you can imagine what happens next (and last)

The Sleepwalking Elevator

Spidery flutterings above cities—handfuls of mica
that reflect your sleek architectures
where there's fighting, there's talk,
there's dancing—why not?

The whole world's tall chimneys
erected on so many slant facets!
pink and white names
scatter like petals
to the four corners of suitcases
I am in the elevator rising to overseas ardors
at the summit of verticals
up there, no more tourists no more bustling
but clouds' love letters that pass by
light and ecstatic

In posh districts overlooking the ocean
they eat salads and scold their servants
who, sheltered in vast kitchens, stuff themselves
no one wants to be lost in space
and become an infinitesimal point
glittering far from the hubbub
there too in saints' eyes as they converse
on Flemish chapel altarpieces

Glorious thrones of our fine feelings
how you buzz
it could be the noble prayer of larches
from my sentimental watchtower.

Old Conversations

He had remembered old conversations with this one and that
  one,
Viaticums which seemed to him to be past use,
In a room almost entirely occupied by a baby grand piano
While in the middle of the square a streetlight crackled,
A little square, German and western, in a pine-tree's shade,
But especially on the bench at Greenwich,
The sky immense, dusk falling
On the line of poplars bordering the lawn
Where children played football, people walked their dogs,
As a few old men strolled before returning to the close air
And medicinal odor of their rooms,
And a biplane descended towards a neighboring club.
Mim had told him one had to be able to talk about oneself
Or one would end up talking about nothing else,
The former breaker of hearts from Moscow to Czernowitz,
The guitarist with chestnut curls and a childish pout,
At present a little man approaching fifty,
Stooped, with an émigré's timid smile,
With his cabled sweater, his bargain boots,
The bitter fatalism of someone who's known hope,
Has seen it grow and fly away
Leaving him alone with his risky, if not pitiful present,
The two-room apartment in a working-class suburb, the pursuit
  of fees,
The candle-end economies,
The son who stayed in the old country, the daughter who left,
The wife hardened by betrayal and neglect,
Showing by every word and gesture
That it is too late to start over,
Content to drift without resistance
And with an infinite patience

For what has she to expect that she hasn't already lost,
Even Grad, pacing the apartment from end to end,
Probably already invaded by metastases,
Had shown reticence.
One does not try to escape the Almighty's will with impunity,
Even in embarking for far-away places.
By stretching over the sheet-music and giving in to sleep,
He had gotten his fingers burnt—
No one else here, between the Hôpital St-Louis and the Institut
Curie
Had had the guts to do it—
And no one would be saved without embarking on the same
road,
Bitter, hard.

Tourists

From Bergen they write: we'll be back before the holidays,
we miss you,
from the Côte d'Azur: it's hard to love by proxy
but still
why this silence?
We get up at dawn
as our parents did
coffee and unintelligible conversations
have their advantages.
Thinking of you
we contemplate the mosaic of sun and sea
till dusk when the moon traces a road
for the last fishermen
history speaks to us as much as nature does
in Rome it's hotter than at home.
Tirelessly, distance plays
its melancholy minuet.

The Terrace

He watches the terrace through the window, that interpreter
he no longer has any claims on the life that bursts and flows
beyond it
down those lanes in view
among palm trees, cork-oaks, mimosas
set there beneath the mauve sky and the blinded sun
doves startled by the gardening operations
flee in a feathered flurry
then calm returns and they are soon heard cooing in the
    branches
this simplicity the predictable course of things which make up
    time
escape his grasp
he sees the balustrades and iron railings
yellow stains on a white ground
or white on yellow
he still has uncertainties and illusions
swiftnesses
the frame reassures him
it fixes the room his gaze as well
which would otherwise wander restlessly
the table composes itself
with the brioche the cup the Chinese earthenware teapot
the sugar bowl the kelp-colored bunch of grapes
the egg-cup and its delicate shadow
on the azure-striped ground of the tablecloth
he thinks he can also see there that shell
he found one morning at the beach
haloed with gold
which he ran to bring back to the house and show
to his sisters and the old governess
who has slept for so many years now above another sea.

The Builder

In memory of J. Ch. S.

There was everything to say that quiet morning
and the silence placed, grown large, behind the door
said it all: each minute was full, shimmering
like a drop of water

childhood spoke through the boy's wide eyes
as the creaking swing in the garden rocked him,
willing prisoner of an endless Sunday,
in wonder, dreaming in the amber string of days

little by little the linden took shape in his vision
dropping its fruits, or rather granting them
to the earth which spring was softening
the façade crumbled, glistening, but darkness broke through,
undulated here and there,

other fires reddened in the depths
hidden from view by heaps of coal
which also served as bulwarks for the nocturnal witch,
beloved, announced by neighborhood watchdogs barking

demons tamed by hands as old as they were skilled
shaped patiently by kneading dough and flesh no less tender
ranged now with objects so numerous they spilled out every-
where
bathed in eternity's blue dust, since that which is past, which
passes, remains

the Kobolds risen from the house's entrails
once obsequious, now unleashed

were concocting, under the cast-iron lid,
a meal to feed the master of the house

seated alone in the vast room where the sun liked to play
he watched sparrows hopping beyond the French windows
embroidered them endlessly in mental needlework
(and later, facing the great gray mountains, they would move
him
even more, he would speak to them like companions)

despite the rips, perpetual wounds
which no thread would mend, which unstitched themselves
nightly
to recreate themselves each morning, torn
resistant to the miracle of the new

pretended metamorphosis in a ball of unbreakable glass
to which only birds brought a new note
a fan of nuances
like Alexandre-François Desportes' toucans in the museum at
Orléans

unfathomable creatures he questioned with a kindly look
expecting no response but the concentrated joy of their move-
ments
What secret order did they obey in their apparent caprice?
What ceremony's unchanging ritual were they enacting?

Unchanging! Like all the rest once time's cloudy layer was
crossed
it unraveled but remained itself.
The women served and cleared the table silently
once the mother's seat was empty, the wife not having joined
him

he also fell silent
coming in, one heard only silverware clinking on plates, moved
with solemn slowness
the sadness he radiated like an ice stalactite chilling a grotto
only lifted once a week

during the Sabbath prayers
when several rows of chairs were set from wall to wall
and the Ark covered with a velvet curtain had left its corner

and the faithful come from neighboring hillsides
lit by the joy with which the canticles throb
old and familiar
made windowpanes tremble chanting the refrains in chorus

on other days though, with what haste, what relief
he went back to his office shaded by the beech above the kennel
where the dog yapped as if alerted
how close the man was who had always been kind to him,
though his intelligence could not grasp the reason

or rather his foundling cur's heart whose gratitude never ran
dry as the years passed
the man seated himself behind the solid wooden table with its
red leather top
caressed for a moment the antique telephone
regained his balance in the world around him

and on this rock…

The Golden Age

Everything is rare in this delicate kingdom
fruit and sealing-wax
silk as well as steel.
A bouquet of flowers
costs more than what would fill a purse
the dead, like the living, must do without.
On sunny days
—which are numbered also—
ladies go out, their parasols in hand
they stroll beside the canals
till the hour when the reddening sun scissors their silhouettes
then erases them like a repentant painter.
Behind the latticed windows, people play music
while drinking wine.
Spinet or lute accompanies the passer-by
who feels an inexplicable pang.
Memories of lace are rustling everywhere
and the swan's dawn cry
freezes forever.

More News of Mr. Nobody

Mr. Nobody's Travels

Sneaking in again, Rovigo tacks to the cork-board
a note intended for Mr. Nobody, who leans on the bar
his whisky diluted with tap-water
he wavers between waking and sleeping, servitude and freedom,
hope and desire thinking to be done once and for all
with that spider-web called "reality,"
to let himself go to get to the other side
with its stretch of vermilion beaches
and glistening dark thickets
which shelter elves and fauns
where a lyre sounds which, till now, he has known only by
hearsay.

*

Walking along the row of yew-trees
Mr. Nobody thinks of his old patronym

a name destined for chronic sorrow
and drink

he sees those hotel rooms again
the damp-stained wallpaper

the smudged panes
which diffused a permanent false daylight

Copenhagen, Göteberg, Bremen

now, pedaling in a white suit
between the blood-drops of bayberries

he understands—relieved—that things had merely followed
their natural order
owing nothing to "self-control" or "the triumph of the will"
and other nonsense of that sort

The Incarnations of Mr. Nobody

I was with two women in the cemetery at Malines
poplars were rustling above our heads
the Flemish lion flapped against the gray sky
I was walking along the railroad tracks a pointer trotting beside
 me
as I whistled a ballad whose lyrics I'd forgotten
my father killed himself there one Christmas night
I would think of him each time I passed that way
but without grief or anger
I, Rosenvige, Dutch botanist,
planted fir trees in Greenland's inhospitable soil
after a few weeks, I went back to Holland
and soon caught up in other projects, other journeys
I forgot my trees given up to the far north's bitterness
in the interest of science
I woke in the middle of the night in a luxurious hotel room
drenched in silence and in burning solitude
at the counter of a bar in Hampstead
I wrote an elegy on beer-glass rings
which I mislaid the next day while taking a walk
when I thought I heard time's melodious racket
like my ancestors, I cultivated a vineyard
that gave an iris-scented wine with bluish highlights
I made miniature furniture for Petronella Oortman
boy running barefoot toward the horizon's call
I crossed a field and then some meadows
followed at a distance by a big black horse

Mr. Nobody Joins the Broken Hearts Club

One of them has kept his love intact
with its shimmerings and chasms
another gets rid of it the way he'd throw away a withered plant
sweeping away even the last crumbs of earth
scattered on the balcony
while the third one separates the object from its attributes
and keeps watching the chimney-pots
at dusk,
keeps drinking, at his kitchen table,
the black gritty wine of an unknown south
—and how should I behave,
Mister Nobody asks himself
having stopped at a café
where he had—he remembers now—
once desired and then broken things off
between two journeys
although crossings would probably be a more appropriate word
    under the circumstances
which example to follow
but he ought perhaps to choose them in turn
mix everything up or even innovate why not
or (on the other hand) take advantage of the occasion
to lay out his thoughts
try to decipher time's secret meaning
explore psychic space in all its dimensions
to recount (and understand)
genealogies and sequences
then he pockets his notebook again
notices that the waiters have piled up the chairs
that he is the last client of the night
that they are waiting impatiently for his departure
leaving just one ceiling lamp lit above his head
which shines on his glass his pen his hands with their bitten nails.

Mr. Nobody Speaks to His Voice

Voice, you sprouted like a shrub
year after year:
I remember your first fragility,
touching frailty they'd do anything to protect
then the sudden, succeeding roughness
with a vigor no one would have thought you had.
Where was the foliage of your songs and cries?
You were naked then as those black skeletons lined up on
winter roads
between snow-covered fields.
When you cradled infant ears and the exquisite ones of the
beloved
bringing sleep to one and the other
it seemed you had reached your golden age
which, like the poets, you thought would never end.
But soon noises still unknown to you, pleas, moans, sighs
glided into you like hands into someone else's gloves.
As well as you could, you put up with them, you claimed them,
they became your attributes, your weapons,
and other women murmured that you were gentle
in the night after love's long commotion.
When the time comes when you tremble like a string
that has shot its arrow towards the target,
when you are chipped, crumbled, broken,
when you caw, croak pitifully,
console yourself, tell yourself that at the end of the cold, dark
corridor
shines your immortal soul: silence.

Mr. Nobody and the Theater

If he could, Mr. Nobody would have written plays,
would have done nothing but that, ready, he tells himself,
to drop everything, his family—reduced, it's true
to a sister living in another hemisphere,
the hydrangea on his balcony,
and his beloved translations from the Aramaic.
Characters appear to him, then disappear
to be replaced by others, some return.
All these strangers are now—and really,
from the moment they take shape in his mind—well-known to
him,
more than that, are his children,
at once his doubles and unlike him,
children who will never change,
will perpetually wear the same clothing,
whom nothing will dislodge from the park bench, from the win-
dow,
from the parlor of an inn
or from an empty neon-lit room colored only by a red blind—
he sees them do outdated dance steps,
he hears them quarrel and reconcile, evoke their memories,
exchange impressions, tell each other the world's news,
sometimes a joke,
strike up sea-chanties or marching songs,
and love songs, especially, with flowers, birds, fountains.
Oddly, he never invents plots for them;
in their mouths he puts languages which feed his fantasies,
Italian, Danish, Polish,
and, when you think of it, it is his dreams as well as theirs
woven together
which would best animate (or perturb) the unwritten works
that he sees as clean sheets
hung on a clothesline
above new grass sprouting in a springtime garden.

Mr. Nobody's Allergies

Mr. Nobody, no longer young, develops an allergy to tuna;
he discovers this by accident
in an Italian restaurant in the historic city center.
His face turns red, his eyes go bloodshot
his table-mates push their chairs back, terrified,
say a doctor should be called immediately
but Mr. Nobody categorically refuses all aid
and staggers toward the men's room
where he plunges his head into the toilet bowl.
He has barely recovered from his first attack
when a second occurs,
even worse
which keeps him flat on his back for several days.
Despite a meticulous reconstitution of his liquid and solid
intake,
he arrives at no convincing explanation,
and Mr. Nobody wonders if it wasn't the environment which
had provoked his illness this time.
He suspects the pigeons in the square where, when the weather
permits,
he goes to sit and read the evening newspaper,
the neighbor's cat who mysteriously prefers his terrace crowded
with worm-eaten boxes and rusty metal chairs
to her mistress's, planted with flowers
or it could be the dying cypress tree behind the Augustine
monastery,
last vestige of a departed park.
Then, during a cruise on the Nile on the luxury yacht
Ferdinand de Lesseps
where there were no animals, and not the smallest shrub,
and he ate only bread and rice due to a case of dysentery he'd
contracted the very afternoon of his arrival

an attack twice as virulent as the one he'd suffered in the restaurant
made him suddenly understand the multifaceted nature of his ailment:
the sources of his pathology were numerous;
and the most surprising among them,
discovered empirically on the upper deck
on the occasion of an evening of Viennese waltzes
was women. Not a certain type of woman,
no, women in general.
One must add that men irritated him almost equally,
and there, too, of whatever sort.
Only children, babies especially, and the very old, sunk in their wheelchairs
seem to lack the element his organism rejects so violently.

Mr. Nobody as the Last Mountaineer

In the Destiny Motel, Mr. Nobody carefully reworks the last act
of a play begun six decades earlier in an African country
beneath its flags and lime-whitened acacias.
It's the longest comedy in history
he lived it, embodied it, staged it day after day
but now, though he gave it everything, it looks him in the eye
and laughs in his face.
Mr. Nobody has turned on the television which at this hour broadcasts only
game-shows whose prizes are electrical kitchen appliances, paltry sums
or spouses for lasting relationships.
From the window of his room he sees the vesperal flow of traffic
partially blanked-out billboards on the other side of the highway
(with amusing results like Nootel or Koak)
and a euphemism for nature in the grassy road-shoulder pecked by crows.
He has shaved, put his bridegroom's suit back on, and the dress-shoes he's polished.
A bottle of Condrieu, and Balzac's *Une ténébreuse affaire* occupy the little corner table
meant for a telephone.
Unless he's missed something, he's convinced he constitutes the entire clientele of this establishment
so thorough is the silence.
He glimpses a sheet of letterhead paper and jots a question on it:
By whom would I like to be greeted?
And the answer: La Fontaine.
He slips the paper, folded in quarters, into an envelope he leaves prominently visible on the bolster

then he stretches out and closes his eyes.
The next day, he describes the scene in detail to his analyst, Dr.
Friedel
who shakes his hand effusively as if he were the sole survivor of
a Himalayan expedition.

Riverbend Passage

The Black Streets

The soldiers on their way to besiege the mountain
stopped here to let blue wine blot out
steaming blood
the devil spoke to them
not the one who watches over the old synagogue
or sets the nuns of St. Peter's dancing behind their high convent
 wall
a demon with no qualms about poor peasants
it's the end of summer
the ploughmen had no time to harvest
nor the vintners to pick grapes that rot now on the hillside
he has brought them this far
and wants to keep climbing
but no flesh matches his ardor

you will not know

you will not know
the days of smoke and frost
the rows of trees with their hands up

you will not know
the growing realm of night,
tardy, cheerful mother

you will not know
the waiting, men like beasts
in the interstices

Pacifics

This man is not the last one
here he is, kept, finally
the cold chased him from day to day
he'd like to marry the sun!
women who watch him pass by
give him affectionate names
without ever trembling
how blonde the light is today
around him
how blue the peaks are
the world perfects itself beneath his eyes
he has forgotten the dreary straddlings
no longer feels the stiffness of his limbs

*

Nothing unfolds on your old life's horizon
where every hour rings out desertion
open water beneath your steps could make you shiver
if your blood responded
tonight you'd like to laugh while draining hope's cup
you know you won't give up any more
than the impassioned sinner
who sees the world in the light of his vice
does a merciful smile await him
at the highest window?
The sky unfurls its stars one by one
you are already dreaming of roses
brilliant with impatience
but the diamond's fire is a legend

*

The soul's sky never clears
even in brilliant mornings' summer clarity
all night long the sources were turning over their soil
and founding an existence
the days stretch out their endless cities
but the sky promises lightness
and launches its swallows
so that children can touch them
in squares where dusk struggles with the chestnut trees
(they're uprooting them now from the pavement, and soon from
   your heart)
sometimes you kneel
you accept your crossed shadows on the hillside
companions of the donkey bearing his load down the path
with angelic steps

*

There is more than that vast, tawny happiness
the evening turns metallic, smoke climbs up
eyes are like prisms
blinking with hope
each industrious mile brings us closer
your night is unconquered
it opens slowly on the world's beach

And I Killed Them All

1.
at dawn with fifty men—the best ones—we entered the village
and we slit everyone's throat, even the cattle

2.
the mothers walked down the road their children in their arms
when they had no strength left to continue and could walk no
further they were shot

3.
the men sixteen years of age or over were bound hand and foot
with barbed wire and dragged across the swamps

4.
no one escaped our detachment's zone of action some were
slaughtered where they lived the rest in the abandoned fodder
silos

5.
we had been informed that the members of a family were re-
turning from the city after a wedding we therefore set up a road-
block and when they arrived I gave them the order to get out of
the car to line up at the edge of a field and I killed them all

The Drownings in the Yonne

In memory of Frédéric B.

*

sometimes, you know it, the wheat spears are as blue
as the deep perspectives
of old buildings
at nightfall

and sometimes, tired of stretching vainly toward the sun
they lie down on ridged earth
refusing to move

if you cross the bridge, you will find
a jutting ash tree
washing its wounds in the current

faces call from between the fishing boats
whose flanks beat ceaselessly against the bank
ghost at the edge of an abyss of light

*

see me my Lord how I am straying
like the lamb condemned to the slaughterhouse I pass through
  doorways
above which lanterns lead me on with their single eye
I cross steel bridges that tremble
each time a train rolls beneath their bellies
you were born in winter
among old trees surrounded by stones
I climb toward pallid places where night and day are squabbling
  in different

distant languages
the city would like to entice me into a dream
decked in garlands in honor of your star
but I take my life away deep into the alleyways

*

a voice rolls down to the trough of the waves
the chimes did not sound
how to lay one's head on a motherly breast?
the drowned room keeps shining
what do we know besides
the old fecundity

The Fire Within the Sanctuary Walls

1809: Napoléon's invasion of Slovenia

Nameless soldier, vast and solitary
under the lindens of Laibach
freedom wrenched you from the plough's yoke
you left home
gave your little sisters a farewell kiss
stroked the damp muzzles of cattle you would never see again
freedom's call was powerful
it resounded unceasingly in your ears
on the roads of Burgundy and Beauce
Paris promised everything to the sons of France
blades were planished, cannons were cast
for you and your multitudes
on Sunday in church
priests glorified Country before praising God
base recruiting officers who forgot their vows
and young women peered at you in your fine uniform
their prayer-books face-down on their knees
soon the troops would be set in motion:
the march toward the east was beginning.

*

A new hope was steaming beneath the rain
the road twisted alongside the Karst
with border-guard horizons behind it
fever was the enemy that could not be battled
unreeling the army of heroes
the dying pawed the earth like wild boars
who then would have dared sing the new hymns?
Fires lit for the hunt went whistling out
mocked by small birds hidden in thick-leafed branches

one day a far-off horn sounded:
it was calling lost dogs home.
Some heard the last judgment in it
they waited for the sea to render up the departed
others took respite from fatigue
on the bench of an inn on the bank of a stream
to the right they wrapped vegetables in straw, to the left, they lit
torches
the season schemed away from night
faces glued to windowpanes gorged on contemplation of the
fields
that would be scythed tomorrow, grand village festival,
all of nature would dry out between now and then
the grass would have flowed back, and the shoals of land—

After the puddles came dust
flies appeared ex nihilo around the horses.
They had to stop on the riverbank,
color of an eternal springtime;
life, recaptured, was born for the last time
of water and spirit
two swallows mimed the future
at the base of a pretty ash-tree
clouds gazed at themselves in the water before dissolving
in storm-droplets
the air welcomed a silvery haze
that cooled the stifling scene
where bitten through by oblique gunfire
only moments later, a drab pile
the remaining bodies
would fall
pierced by a single idea

*

Thus ended the peregrinations of men sure of returning sooner or later to their native land. That certainty, as for all those who preceded them or would come after, would accompany them all through the campaign, and if it had not been, at the beginning at least, incompatible with reality, it acquired, the farther they travelled from their bountiful land, the qualities as well as the failings of a dream: energy, perseverance, obsession, folly. A light as lively as it was deceptive by which they were illuminated while they marched at that cadenced pace which was theirs up till the moment when they were reduced as one to flesh.

Riverbend Passage

Don't let the man in black
take me away with him

cowbells / opera

*

There was once a time when sorrow lay down on me
as if it wished to warm me
truly it troubled my spirit
I was
Biblical

*

The child fears water and bees
he watches helicopters winch up cows
his life is you
bicephalous
in the mountain pastures again

*

From Badland to Deadwood
the man is on my heels
don't let him take me away on his black charger
or aboard the black convoy
the interlife express

*

When the sun sets
I will be swallowed
dispersed
blown away in a thousand shards of schist

after our walk you remember
the forest's joyful silence

*

The bird in quarter-view
planted nails
dead trees were my linens
for laying out the dead
I will turn towards life's blue
determined as a bee

*

At the foot of the lightning-blasted tree
lamentation lamentation
descent from the cross hung on the cross
the single bird weeps
the horse strikes its shoe
the father dreams of nature
stopped short

*

In lives' riverbends
willowherb stretches out toward the man walking alone
o sacrifice, o secret
stitches: conjunction

*

Thus the generations continue
and the motionless eagle eyes his prey
down to the pastures' hidden nooks
cowbells
stay restless child
I—we—clouds

*

Clouds
press on us and pray for us forever
nature would weigh nothing
if an angel lifted our fields

*

Age that meat-hook
beyond all the bends
when the miracle of the
procession happens—
hatching, blossoming

*

The King told me
that story
he whelps litters of them

*

I listened to him
and on the way back
I wept silently
I thought I saw
ghost horses
I heard the sun's hugeness
—an opera—
I was magical metamorphosed
the restless child

Études and Elegies

Antibes Elegy

For Laura

How to tell simply of this return
which was neither that of the prodigal son
nor of Ulysses to his homeland
but more like a death and a resurrection
seagulls were being born from the rain
mountains unfurled their snowy peaks
like banners of welcome
sailboats were dashing towards the horizon
skimming the water with their ropes and cables
the shadows lined up along the avenues
were not gathered there for us
indifferent as they were to our passage
yet I recognized without hesitation
the swimming instructor the grocer the man from the tree nursery
the neighbor woman the ice-cream vendor
perhaps they were waiting for other ghosts
the same ones whom we hoped to see appear at the doorway
at the far end of the row of trees or on the terrace
while only the cypress hedges welcomed us
and the early jasmine

First Elegy

Frédéric Chopin, 17 October 1849

On all the world's mountaintops, no love...
A body cachectic and blotched
with the world's wear and tear.
Where had the heart gone?
O voices of plain-chant
O real
rising toward eye-blue stained glass where a dove
spreads an enigma's wings
between two discreet roses!

The body had been profaned
its viscera studied nocturnally
by a band of medical students
come from the east
they had come barefoot through the dust of Silesia
humming old ballads
The heart torn out
embalmed
hidden in a basket of eggs
and taken across the border river

lost in the snow one day then found again
filched by God's conjurors
presented repeatedly by charlatans
at county fairs
before disappearing
sole passenger
and cargo of a vessel on the high seas
that was the body loved so often by the same hands faithful to each member

the multiple body rain-battered
at the song-thrush's flight

Second Elegy

The assassins had all gone back to barracks
their helmets remained, piled with their banners
as on the eve of a battle

What are those shadows beneath the tree of life?
Holy women, swooning, faces bathed with tears,
your eyes reflect the last sunset's gold
gone to lose itself in the last sea's crevices.

Only an old man is left
to unfold the sheet
as smooth to the touch
as love between brothers and sisters
even those born to different fathers or different mothers.

A slow cortège emerges from the city gates
where houses are rose-colored, palaces snowy.
Night shrouds its movement
despite the torches brandished above the catafalque.
Ghostly horses
hooves wrapped in cloth to muffle the sound
pull the carriage surrounded by old soldiers.
The procession staggers under the oaks
No one will return from this entombment.

Man of sorrows
you will bloom like the lily
you will triumph
liberating mystery
and the stone will have rolled away a hundred times
from the door to your tomb

The hook pulling the weeds
from the ploughshare
is what you will be
the stranger come to the shearing
is what you will be
the salt which dyes the colorless fabric
royal purple
is what you will be
bright line crossing the symbol-circle of flowers
is what you will be

First Étude

Stop for a moment in front of the Farnese Hercules
or the portrait of Balthazar Castiglione
Have they ever looked at one another?
And could they?
Representation: capture, recovery, concretion
they are simpler and more advanced than we are
like a figure at the end of the pier
body already bent toward the waves
they are halfway there
a perfect image
                                        a reflection
offered for our admiration
we claim that they respond to the plea in our eyes
that they are brought to life by our seeing them
that a painted or sculpted figure
stared at intensely
stares back at you
thus twice created
absence become matter and matter brought to life
fruits of vision
we'd be entitled to expect from them
that revolution that self-examination
which would make of them objects within the object
existing both as entity and symbol
of the boundary between interior and exterior
insurmountable wall
which prevents us from observing ourselves
from weighing on, weighing in against ourselves
poor subjects
perpetual vanishing-points
never sustained but lit up here and there
where weakness touches them

Second Étude

We end up knowing one thing, then another
we've raised simplicity's flag without really believing in it
because our complexity is unknown, not understood
we'd have to speak like a dying man
like someone on a station platform who
is taking leave of his beloved forever
and has thirty seconds before the train leaves
I'm not so sure
and the more I think about it
my back against the paneled wall of this plush hotel bar
where we would get morosely and methodically drunk
if you were here, my love
the more I'm convinced of the opposite
and I'd like to lower the flag
simplicity has its virtues
it gives the hulls of boats their pastel colors
on a sea drawn by a child's hand
perhaps it sketches a smoking chimney nearby
and on the charging soldier's lips
places a gay
and slightly sentimental song
it sends a fire truck rushing at full speed
towards its daily good deed
but—the heart with its facets sharper than a diamond's
the subtle, unpredictable play of light on water
the system of grief, the system of joy
how can it do more than stand silently beside them?

Third Étude

Another time, and with it, a different music
like two conversations, unrelated
except that one voice is common to the two
an unknown presence behind the curtains
behind the familiar façade
an untouchable past
risen from a gray, rainy day
a voice says don't pull the shadows from their sleep
and you defer to it
but then, who disturbs them?
Who makes them tremble?
The bells of another time call out elsewhere
they weave their own hours
above the synagogue which is our real sky
are they deceitful because of that?
He who drinks down autumn, who is made of seasons
is walking perhaps amongst even more mirages
while a present which the order to return might salvage
marks out its dissonant line

Fourth Étude

What is this life that runs alongside life
or overflows it
life as it passes
along the limits
a rare occasion, I think
to show it those parts
of itself it usually can't see
as if you could—at last—glimpse your own back
or your eyes
see what escapes and establishes us
that quality of sleep
I was going to write that matter
for it is entirely
and exclusively
matter
of a sleep that cannot be interrupted
even during those exceptional moments
when light crosses and reverses it

But we, as we take a walk between two fields
on a little country road
to put our thoughts in order, draw up the balance sheet
of our acts and years
if a voice said to us
"you are not walking, you are sleeping"
we would take offense, we would deny it
we would hasten our steps
hearing an accusation
where there was an invitation

Fifth Étude

In the ring, a clown apes love
two goats with gold-ribboned horns
bleat to emphasize the parody
the audience claps wildly in the name of non-love
but stubborn desire
which comes from the anus and ends up there
let him just try miming that!

When you push open certain doors
you find nothing: no walls, no ceilings
no floor on which to plant your feet
and yet hearts once beat in bedrooms

a secret weighs on this emptiness
the secret of a beginning
predating the first word
of an insult dating back
to fields slashed and burned in the shadow of castles

since then a hot rain has been burning away
falling obliquely on the southern slope
which the pilgrim climbs distractedly
guided by a crow

he hopes for neither salvation nor ruin
lets the incessant rain soak him through
he feels neither hunger nor thirst
only the dim need
born in him
an origin a dread a gnawing
the tree of life

Sixth Étude

Eye-water, white water
places named by hearing
before being seen
(and you sleep in a dilation of presence)
as the plants give thanks
as the maguey cactus greet
the drowned men's bridge
where the drowned men's source
cracks the landscape
I want nothing less than the infinite
from an expected adverb
the sliding tongue steals between the lips
laundress of the teeth
on washing night
when the village women gather on the bank
of the Aztec-named river
with strange birds
called *tordos* here
a kind of crow
eternal neighbors of the *opilotes*
language must remain
our precious native fabric
how a landscape becomes landscape
and a language, landscape
a road lined with crosses and sown with corpses
splits my tongue
I go two ways at once
I love I smooth
the vast nocturnal cloth

Funeral Supper

I. M. Stéphane Moses

Man had straight forward gone / To endlesse death....
George Herbert

Dismantling

Pallid objects tear apart the brain
that has floated down a thousand streams
Who notices the slow-worm
just before an evening's fanfare?
A kind of gallantry cocooned the preparation of the body
it dreamed among the women
even its washed feet wandered off in the color-bursts
of glass that sadden statues kneeling on ancient wood
O irreversible heart
prey of the poorest—shivering clowns outside the hospice door
how I longed for a ray of pure light through the curtains
and on the tablecloth

*

The frost—this Morning—
wakes the stones, wakes death
(how we dance beneath their feet!)
they rise towards the plumed sky....
Nothing is waiting here:
no more laughter at the table than in echoes of snow
A tune accompanies the spheres' trot round the ring

*

Haphazard in that last state where you are settling
unsettling—flutter particolored
pieces shrunken down to edges

They murdered the singers O old troubadors
they came to get them one by one

Who speaks of the marriage of virgins and fools
The ancestors, church-restorers
from the banks of the Meuse
to Algiers of the Jews...

*

A day in February '77

It would have taken one single love
like the single figure in the latrines that day
We wished each other the best of luck
pushed by fate
who was it who needed whom

At last hours covered the earth

*

From a family album

Tipped from another ox-cart
again and again into the alfalfa
that fathered and mothered you
your breath glistened in the lantern-light
those evenings gaily gliding
between the Bug and the Vistula

*

From an album found by chance

Large tracks, chevron-patterned
the other signs also kept their distance
from darkened hearths and trees

it all was nameless
the stones did not have your face
you would have slept at the foot of the well
on a bed of hay
too much frost was steaming there
for language to intervene in
the boy's endless march
just after the war
his endless history
boat on a backdrop of burning

*

The hour has come   Show yourself
pilgrim beneath the sky's arcades
a staircase rose towards corbelled balconies
the heart walked backwards

You had nothing to hold to
but a canteen-woman
widow and widow's daughter
You had to make love to her
at dawn before the battle

when the elms rose one by one
days' sentinels

*

My utter gold
helmet aflame with solitude
a forger found his descendants
at the mouthpiece where birds pause
(they dance this morning like tawny snowflakes)
I remember a Nativity of joy joy joy
how the sky crystallized
oboes celebrated

Child disturbed by gravity
Feverish with this vast inheritance

*

Epilogue

The doctor said to me: your skin is crying for you
I thought—tears of blood
love was another place of mourning
medieval village rich with symbols
to which Compassion had laid waste
in the doctor's eyes the body's language
spoke Hope

Alive

At the hour when the world ceases to be
you will be sitting under a plane-tree half unleafed
on a lively, noisy avenue
nothing around you will have really changed
you will still be father, son and lover
a dream will nag you like a bit of food lodged between two teeth
you will go on watching children, cyclists, dogs
asking yourself what love is
if you found it, lost it, or if it always escaped you
examining memories attentively
with an entomologist's precision, who, bent over an insect,
now sees only reticular surfaces
forgetting the creature caught in a fog-drowned park
you will think of the fruits in season, of buying a new pair of
shoes
of the page you read this morning in the bathtub
of the windowpanes next door lit up as if on fire
which you watched for a long time last night before going to bed
and of light's tenderness when you awoke
which seemed to stretch the sky
extend it to infinity
at the hour when the world ceases to be
you'll do sums, review hypotheses
formulated a thousand times
summon up the solutions
then you'll get up, distractedly push two or three leaves aside
with your foot
you'll move away towards nothing
your back turned on nothing
so alive

The Music That
Set Him On This Road

Julius Bissier Played the Cello

In his diary, the German painter Julius Bissier writes:
"As a spider surprises us in dreams, in sleep,
dread grips my throat" (November 13, 1943)
and on January 16, 1944:
"Immeasurable strength is needed to wait for life's rebirth."

Taken at the same period, a photograph shows him
playing the cello
equally attentive, it seems, to sounds drawn from the instrument
and to internal resonances
his face divided between light and shadow.

Each day he calls out to the infinitely distant
which answers him personally.

Poems for You in Istanbul

Why do certain nights
                    crack open
while others are smooth as obsidian mirrors
—oh, your peasants in their earthen houses
                    open to all comers
oh, the stray dog whom you alone loved—?
if my glance wandered worried like a lookout's
                    climbing the mast in ocean fog
excuse me
I go down the cloud-marked path again
I whistle among trees trembling with joy
my breath grows within me
and gives me a Titan's skin

*

Where were you
perhaps on the Istanbul-Salonica Express
or in the train station buffet
perhaps atop the Galata Tower
perhaps with the cats in the marketplace
I looked for you among the sad fishermen on the bridge
in the ragged crowds at the cloth market
I had only love in my mouth
the café waiters laughed under the arbors
I thought I recognized you in the Virgin's face
beneath Hagia Sophia's gilt firmament
you were all the faces
the Anatolian farm woman's under her multicolored scarf
the pharmacist's as she took an old couple's blood pressure
the driver's singing joyfully to her rear-view mirror
you were everywhere
passing by
sitting with the little pickpockets

Saint John of the Past

Saint John of the past
what passion in the blaze
fed by rosemary branches
luckily they pulled you out
at the last moment

at the edge of the ocean
each overturned stone
proclaims the ancient presence
a lamb has conquered death
by dying in the soaked grass
after a violent storm
God would seat him on his own blue throne
where you still see him
in childhood's bedroom

Cathedral of the Holy Cross, Orléans

There was an enormous snowy space around the cathedral
it was emptiness as sentinel
was it a song renewed century after century? about the triumph
of heroes covered by a bed of dust?
A black welcome broached no inkling of the towers
where the sky cut out idealized foliage
I was cold, and powerful stone arms
seized me, sheltered me with so many others
those perennial workers' arms
with sieges' saltpeter still powdering their skin
oh all those winters surrendered to soldiers
—the snowflakes transfigured—
repentant shadows were gliding between the pews.

Note from Burgundy

the bush burnt to ash
is more of a gossip than ever
all the neighborhood passes by
from canal-lock to bell-tower
diluting however slightly its blackness
in the season's illumination

Poems on the Island

Majorca, 2004

Mimosa at Picafort

They were the last of the season
copper had replaced gold
they confined themselves to roadsides
and vacant lots
disdained by newer blossoms
who would pluck them now
besides a few children tired of playing,
an old man, to brighten his old wife's
sickroom?
insects no longer approached them
they seemed vaguely ashamed
to be there still
tarnishing the foliage
while they knew they were expected elsewhere
and wished perhaps to be there already
they alone through those days of indecision
accepted their lot with resignation
the sea foamed
the sky thundered
the wind braced itself
like a huge horse
brought by force to the island
they still had everything to give
to any hurt heart

Between Waking and Sleeping

In this place of reconciliation where time bends and is scattered
ducks fly above the reeds
when you reach the old factory
the song of women planting rice still rises
with the tawny owl's cry

green and silver, the water no longer reflects knees
and the shadows have fled
sometimes you find bygone faces
beneath wrinkled masks
in gloomy flats on the outskirts of resorts
but delicate clover crowns
protect these paddocks of servitude
and evening lights them up like Christmas candles
thrusting from thickets of digitalis

for anyone who loses his way often
these ruts have no secrets
beyond the little bridge are other territories
which keep up their own legends
of amorous metamorphoses
sleeping maidens take warning
when the osprey arrives

Faunesque

Their heads flame with death and love
you abandon them on park benches
where animality
feasts forever

but the city spills out something else
a rain of translucent names
through which can be seen
the imperial blue sky
the night the Pleiades on a canopy

pillage in side-chapels and tomb-niches
the nave still held thousands of hurried footsteps
the birds flew away once and for all
no need for the watchmen to ascend
the tower each morning
the sea will no longer bear witness
to great migratory flows

the pirates' flag at the Savior's feet
calls up the gathered martyrs
their bones dance with Bacchantes
around the Parilla of the besotted
heading straight for coitus

Café Lirico

Farewell to your villages of rose-scented soap
my lyric island
to your lemon trees ogling naked women
at poolside
like the elders in Scripture
farewell horses with bandaged pasterns
black pigs sleeping side by side with turkeys
farewell silky, laughing sky
escaped from the mountains' too-brief embrace
farewell thistles farewell poppies
farewell dry stone walls of long-past days
battleships and birds stay in dock
last defenders of the Christian palaces
still haunted by innumerable Sicilian shadows
the call to prayer is stilled the baths are no longer steaming
but the bell-tower still looks towards an incongruous east
with the royal verdigris-tinted angel
in the off-hours the Phoenician and the Greek
exchange gossip in their shop doorways
they tire their eyes searching the horizon beyond the ramparts
neither Rome nor Belisarius will return
farewell to the gems of the bishop's palace
the two silver pomegranates looted from some synagogue
no doubt transformed since into a church or convent
farewell my lyrical cafés

Royal Blue

Something unknown melts beneath our footsteps
the nights have left us nothing
photographs of what occurred are still discussed
but the history which prevails
is that of churches' white roses

*

Crush the fires of Prussia beneath a dark heel
every façade bleeds
bleeding, the trees strip themselves
the people are a flock of steaming pigs
on the way to the sty

*

There shall be no other center but the snow
cut short my breath O greatest light
covering the oaks beneath the old city walls
words doze in the wide sensual bed
where even green sap dares not wake them

The Lacemakers

the lacemakers are no longer in the Pelican
but the Beguines haven't budged from behind their windows
the empress of Constantinople has forgotten them
unlike the thrushes recalling autumn all around them

the lock-keeper has gone too
with Saint Donatien in his brocade coat
of whom any relic is vainly sought
in reliquaries glistening deep in crypts

they slide continually under bridges, flush with the water
passengers in the black skiff
Our Lady shelters them beneath her cloak of piety
when snow falls on the canals and covers the swans
pressed up against the trunks of old willows

Usedom, Baltic Sea

Gulls will greet the strolling players again at the border train-station…
At the beginning of summer, a theater raised its red and white
tent
against the dunes. How the boardwalk livened up at dusk!
Hotels poured out an uninterrupted stream of guests
and rich vacationers emerged from villas to mingle with the
crowd,
thrilled, after their stuffy garden-parties,
to get drunk on cheap beer and savor waffles whose vanilla odor
rising from stands all down the walkway filled the warm air.
Fire-eaters on the esplanade
they came back after the years of shadow
and more than one frozen heart resumed beating
Buggies went off behind the plane trees, privilege of embracing
souls
the carousels tuned vertiginously
whisked away by barrel-organ music
poor spinners at miserable café doorways
bent beneath so much clandestine sorrow

Brandenburg Letters

The bells of my life have rung for me
at last I'll have to push open the little door
I know this garden behind the abandoned house
you can find red clover there and small blue plums
I often walked alone down its rows of trees
during those years of lightness
when, pulled along by clouds
the only ground I noticed was their shadow

*

to my sister

A flower of silence as decoration
surrounded by partitions carved in all good faith
through the openings a curious boy sees virgin
birches
which cinder a sky whose daylight is withdrawing
he walks barefoot to feel soil and grass
later he was taken away to jail

*

My lavender sky closed in a perfume bottle
keeps the secret we confided in it
those days' heat is elsewhere now
just as the torrents of white light are gone
to drown other gardens where desire rises
leaving the tables at the lawns' edges empty

*

To you as well—you'll pardon me—G.S. 7 Anderson Street,
  Chelsea
I write a note

and what does it matter if you don't answer
since "that which was will never cease to be"
thus the hydrangeas two houses over
of which you must have been very fond
and in summer that green eastern shadow
which enveloped almost the whole length of the street

*

He will leave without our having understood
or even recognized each other
I don't know why I'm telling you about that
instead of the redstart on the pine trunk
in early afternoon
extravagance of our breathing
I noticed it all at once
not more or less surprised than by a summer shower

*

Your people shed purple blood
and the usurer became an angel
love letters pile up in the ditch
where the dying take their pleasure without making a sound
while devils celebrate their weddings

Towards Buxtehude

He kept walking
between the poplars and the tarmac
went by farms fields
power stations
cars passed him
black inside
one rainy night he put his foot on something
crunchy and soft:
a run-over hedgehog
thrown by the violence of the impact
onto the road's shoulder
it had begun to snow very early that year
but that didn't discourage him
slowed him down a bit at most
he would sing a psalm or canticle
and had the impression
that a fur shawl
had been wrapped around his shoulders
the innkeepers
unused to seeing clients arrive
at that time of year
made him welcome
he would have a meat pie and a piece of fruit for dinner
sleep in plushy beds
all for a few coins
then would depart again at dawn
across the sleeping white-roofed villages
having forgotten for quite a while
the music that had set him
on this road.

Acknowledgments

Grateful acknowledgment is given to the journals in which these translations first appeared:

Bat City Review: "Old Conversations"

Circumference: "The Terrace," "Mimosa at Picafort," "Between Waking and Sleeping"

Crazyhorse: "you will not know," "Mr. Nobody as the Last Mountaineer," "And I Killed Them All"

FIELD: "First Elegy," "On Ugliness," "Towards Buxtehude," "Mr. Nobody and the Theater"

Two Lines: "Brandenburg Letters," "Riverbend Passage"

Mima'amakim: "Royal Blue"

Pequod: "Faunesque," "Café Lirico"

PN Review (UK): "The Incarnations of Mr. Nobody," "Mr. Nobody Joins the Broken Hearts Club," "Mr. Nobody and the Theater," "Mr. Nobody's Allergies"

Poetry Review (UK): "Second Elegy"

Prairie Schooner: "He and I," "Small i," "It's Late, Miss China," "The Drownings in the Yonne"

Poetry Wales: "Mr. Nobody as the Last Mountaineer," "The Lacemakers"

Versal (Amsterdam): "Poems for You in Istanbul"

Zeek: "Alive," "The Incarnations of Mr. Nobody," "Mr. Nobody Joins the Broken Hearts Club," "Mr. Nobody Speaks To His Voice"